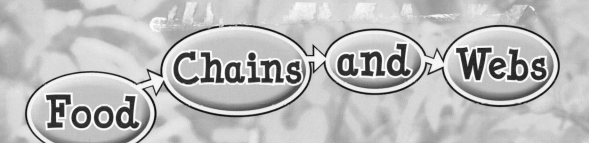

Food Chains and Webs

Rainforest
Food Chains

Angela Royston

D0308911

Raintree is an imprint of Capstone Global Library Limited, a company incorporated in England and Wales having its registered office at 7 Pilgrim Street, London, EC4V 6LB – Registered company number: 6695582

www.raintreepublishers.co.uk
myorders@raintreepublishers.co.uk

Edited by Claire Throp, Diyan Leake and Helen Cox Cannons
Designed by Joanna Malivoire and Philippa Jenkins
Original illustrations © Capstone Global Library Ltd 2014
Picture research by Elizabeth Alexander and Tracy Cummins
Production by Victoria Fitzgerald
Originated by Capstone Global Library Ltd
Printed and bound in China

ISBN 9781 4062 8417 1 (hardback)
18 17 16 15 14
10 9 8 7 6 5 4 3 2 1

ISBN 9781 4062 8424 9 (paperback)
19 18 17 16 15
10 9 8 7 6 5 4 3 2 1

British Library Cataloguing in Publication Data
A full catalogue record for this book is available from the British Library.

Acknowledgements
We would like to thank the following for permission to reproduce photographs: Alamy pp. 11b (© Danita Delimont), 19 (© A & J Visage), 24, 25 chimpanzee (© National Geographic Image Collection), 25 caterpillar (© Nick Greaves), 27 (© imagebroker); Corbis pp. 10 (© Brian A. Vikander), 17 ant (© Mark Moffett/Minden Pictures), 17 lizard (© Stephen Dalton/Minden Pictures), 23a (© Natural Selection David Ponton/Design Pics), 23c, 25 fruit (© Konrad Wothe/Minden Pictures), 25 eagle (© Natural Selection David Ponton/Design Pics), 25 millipede (© Gerry Ellis/Minden Pictures); 26 (© Tim Fitzharris/Minden Pictures), 29 (© Scubazoo/SuperStock); Getty Images pp. 22 (Tim Makins), 25 monkey (Bruno Morandi), 28 (Mark Carwardine); Science Source p. 17 tree (Jacques Jangoux); Shutterstock pp. 1, 13 (© leungchopan), 4 (© Matt Tilghman), 5 (© Jim Leary), 7, 11c, 12 (© Dr. Morley Read), 8 (© javarman), 9, 14, 25 frog (© Aleksey Stemmer), 11a (© Christian Vinces), 15 (© worldswildlifewonders), 17 cobra (© Skynavin), 17 tree snake (© asyrafazizan), 16 (© Microstock Man), 18 (© neelsky), 20 (© Ammit Jack), 21 (© apiguide), 23b, 25 duiker (© Four Oaks), 25 guava (© chai kian shin).

Cover photograph of red-eyed tree frog reproduced with permission of Alamy (© Martin Shields).

We would like to thank Michale Bright for his invaluable help in the preparation of this book.

Contents

Some words are shown in bold, **like this.**
You can find out what they mean by
looking in the glossary.

What is a tropical rainforest?

Most rainforests grow in places that are hot and wet all year round. Tropical rainforests are full of life. Plants grow closely packed together and many trees grow very tall.

Many types of plants grow in rainforests.

A toucan lives among the treetops.

Millions of animals live in the rainforest. Some live on the ground or in the **undergrowth**. Many others live in the treetops. What do they all eat?

Where are the rainforests?

Tropical rainforests grow in hot countries close to the Equator. The map shows where the world's largest rainforests are.

The largest rainforests are marked on the map in dark green.

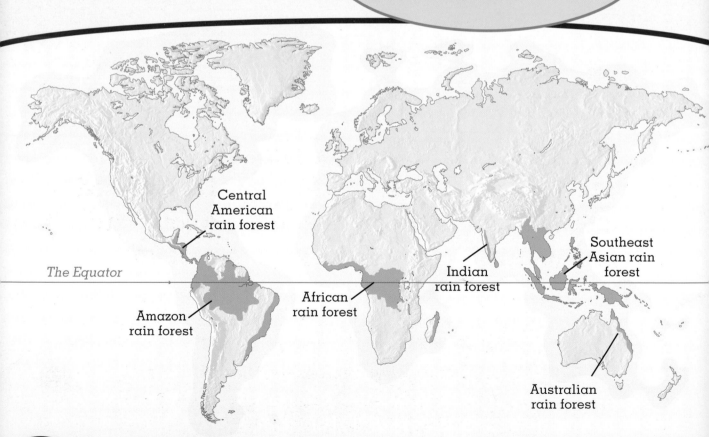

Central American rain forest

The Equator

Amazon rain forest

African rain forest

Indian rain forest

Southeast Asian rain forest

Australian rain forest

The Amazon River flows through the Amazon rainforest.

Rainforests used to be much larger, but people cut down the trees to sell the wood and to farm or mine the land. About half of the rainforests have been cut down.

Biggest rainforest

The Amazon rainforest is the world's largest rainforest. It covers an area about half the size of Europe.

What is a food chain?

A **food chain** shows how food connects animals and plants in a particular **habitat**. The **energy** in food is passed from plants to each of the animals in the chain.

An orangutan uses its feet like hands to move through the trees.

A tree frog clings to a rainforest tree.

Living things need energy to grow and survive. For example, orangutans use energy to swing through the trees. Tree frogs use energy to breathe and to croak.

An Amazon food chain

The **food chain** opposite can be found in the Amazon rainforest. Tapirs eat shrubs and other leaves. **Energy** passes from the leaves to the tapir and then to the jaguar. As the tapir snuffles through the **undergrowth**, it doesn't see the jaguar hiding in the bushes. The jaguar pounces on the tapir and eats it.

Food chain

A jaguar feeds on the tapir

Tapirs eat twigs and leaves

Shrubs grow on the forest floor

Plants and the Sun

The jaguar eats the tapir, but the tapir eats plants. Without the plants, neither animal could survive. All **food chains** begin with plants, because only plants can make their own food.

Green plants make sugar in their leaves.

Bananas grow wild in many tropical rainforests.

Plants are called **producers** because they use **energy** from sunlight to make sugary food. The sugar feeds every part of the plant, including the fruit.

Animal diets

Animals are called **consumers**, because they consume food that they find in their environment. **Carnivores**, such as jaguars and poisonous frogs, hunt other animals. **Herbivores**, such as tapirs and deer, munch on plants.

This frog's blue skin warns other animals that it is poisonous.

A quetzal eats lots of different things.

Many animals eat both meat and plants. They are called **omnivores**. A quetzal, for example, eats mostly fruit, but also catches lizards, frogs and insects.

A Southeast Asian food chain

Most **food chains** have only three or four links, but some food chains are longer. The animals in this food chain all live in the treetops in Southeast Asia. **Energy** passes from the trees to the tree ants and on through the flying dragon and tree snake to the king cobra.

Rainforest in Southeast Asia

Food chain

A tree snake kills
and eats a lizard

A king cobra swallows
a tree snake

A flying dragon lizard
feeds on tree ants

Tree ants feed on
starch from the tree

A tree grows
in the forest

Top predators

The animals at the end of a **food chain** are called top **predators** because they are not hunted by other animals. They include jaguars, tigers and large snakes.

A tiger is a fierce hunter.

A reticulated python is a top predator.

Reticulated pythons are the longest snakes in the world. They coil themselves around prey and choke it to death. Then they slowly swallow their prey whole.

Scavengers and decomposers

Scavengers, such as vultures, are animals that feed on the flesh of dead animals. Some insects lay their eggs in rotting flesh. The eggs hatch into maggots, which then feed on the flesh.

Vultures help to clear the forest of animal remains.

Forest fungi help to break up rotting tree trunks.

Decomposers include worms, insects, fungi and bacteria. Decomposers break up the remains of plants and animals and turn them into soil.

A Congo food chain

The Congo rainforest is the second largest rainforest in the world. In this **food chain, energy** passes from the fruit to the duiker and then to the eagle. The crowned eagle is a top **predator.**

The Congo rainforest

Food chain

An eagle swoops down and snatches the duiker.

A blue duiker eats fruit and leaves.

This fruit has fallen to the forest floor.

Food webs

Most animals belong to several **food chains**. Animals compete for food and may be food for several **predators**. The **food web** opposite is from the Congo rainforest. It shows how food chains link together to form a web.

Chimpanzees eat mainly fruit, but they occasionally eat red colobus monkeys, too.

Food web

crowned eagle

chimpanzee

blue duiker

tree frog

red colobus monkey

fallen leaves and fruit

caterpillar

guava

giant millipede

Important links

Some animals or plants help the whole **habitat.** For example, in Borneo and Sumatra, orangutans wander around, eating fruit and dropping the seeds of many different plants.

A baby orangutan loves to eat fruit.

A cassowary spreads the seeds of large fruit in the Australian rainforest.

The seeds grow into plants which feed many different animals, and so the whole habitat is better off. In places with few orangutans, there are many fewer plants and animals.

Protecting food chains

People are the biggest threat to **food chains**, because they are cutting down the rainforest. For example, in Southeast Asia, the rainforests are being cleared so that palm oil can be grown instead.

Oil palms have been planted in place of rainforest trees and plants.

Big machines have cleared many areas of rainforest.

Unless people work together to preserve the rainforest, the orangutans and other rainforest animals will have nowhere left to live.

Glossary

carnivore animal that eats only the meat of other animals

consumer living thing, particularly an animal, that feeds on other living things, such as plants and other animals

decomposer living thing, such as an earthworm, fungus or bacterium, that breaks up the remains of plants and animals and turns them into soil

energy power needed to do something, such as move, breathe or swallow

food chain diagram that shows how energy passes from plants to different animals

food web diagram that shows how different plants and animals in a habitat are linked by what they eat

habitat place where something lives

herbivore animal that eats only plants

omnivore animal that eats plants and animals

predator animal that hunts other animals for food

prey animal hunted for food

producer living thing, such as a plant, which makes its own food

scavenger animal that feeds off the flesh and remains of dead animals

undergrowth plants in a forest that grow thickly together close to the ground

Find out more

Books

Rainforest (Life Cycles), Sean Callery (Kingfisher, 2011)

Rainforest Food Chains (Protecting Food Chains), Heidi Moore (Raintree, 2010)

Rainforests (Explore!), Jen Green (Wayland, 2012)

Who Eats Who in the Rainforest? (Food Chains in Action), Robert Sneddon (Franklin Watts, 2009)

Websites

www.rainforest-alliance.org.uk/kids
This website for children is all about rainforests.

www.sciencekids.co.nz/sciencefacts/earth/rainforests.html
This website has lots of information and fun facts about rainforests.

www.sheppardsoftware.com/content/animals/kidscorner/games/
foodchaingame.htm
Find out about food chains and test how much you know by playing the food chain game on this website.

Index